B!rds

HOATZIN

by Robin Johnson

A Crabtree Crown Book

Crabtree Publishing
crabtreebooks.com

School-to-Home Support for Caregivers and Teachers

This appealing book is designed to teach students about core subject areas. Students will build upon what they already know about the subject, and engage in topics that they want to learn more about. Here are a few guiding questions to help readers build their comprehension skills. Possible answers appear here in red.

Before Reading:

What do I know about hoatzins?
- *I know that a hoatzin is a type of bird.*
- *I know that hoatzins have spiky feathers on their heads.*

What do I want to learn about this topic?
- *I want to learn about the hoatzin's habitat.*
- *I want to learn about hoatzin chicks.*

During Reading:

I'm curious to know…
- *I'm curious to know why the hoatzin's face is blue in color.*
- *I'm curious to know why hoatzins eat leaves, unlike most other birds.*

How is this like something I already know?
- *I know that many species of birds live in the Amazon rain forest.*
- *I know that some animals give off stinky smells to scare away predators.*

After Reading:

What was the author trying to teach me?
- *The author was trying to teach me about the hoatzin's unique characteristics.*
- *The author was trying to teach me about how the hoatzin compares to other birds.*

How did the images and captions help me understand more?
- *The labels on the picture of the hoatzin pointed out its physical characteristics.*
- *The diagram showed me the parts of the hoatzin's digestive system.*

Contents

Hello, Hoatzin!

Have you ever seen—or smelled—a hoatzin? This odd bird is strange in every sense!

WHAT'S THE NAME?
The word "hoatzin" is pronounced "WAT-sin." Say what now?

HOATZIN BY THE NUMBERS
Length: 26 inches (65 cm) from bill, or beak, to tail
Weight: 2 pounds (1 kg)
Wingspan: 26 inches (65 cm) from wing tip to wing tip
Lifespan: Up to 15 years in the wild

MAKE SENSE OF THE HOATZIN

The hoatzin looks like a pudgy punk-rock chicken.
It is a noisy bird that hoots, squawks, and crashes around in trees.
The hoatzin has a strong barnyard smell.
It tastes as bad as it smells.
It has body parts that feel soft, spiky, or sharp.

Ahem...attention bird lovers!
I am Professor Oddfeather and I will be your
expert guide to the fine feathered friend featured in this book.
I will direct you to amusing facts on odd birds. They really are the
most amazing creatures on Earth. I say this because I am one.
Seriously, I'm a living dinosaur! Look for my instructive
comments throughout the book.

Spot the Hoatzin

A bird this odd and spectacular is not hard to identify. No need for binoculars. Just eyeball it!

A long, spiky **crest** sticks up on its head

A blue face and bright red eyes

A short, strong bill for gripping and ripping tough leaves

Reddish-brown feathers covering most of its stocky, pear-shaped body

Male and female hoatzins look the same—like strange, awkward birds.

Short, rounded wings that allow it to fly—sort of. The hoatzin flies very clumsily for very short distances.

THAT'S CLAW-SOME!
Like all birds, hoatzins have claws on their toes. But hoatzin chicks also have claws on their wings! They use the claws for climbing until they can fly, which is when the claws come off.

A long, stiff tail that it uses for balance in the trees

The scientific name for the hoatzin is *Opisthocomus hoazin*, which means "long hair behind."

Where in the World?

Hoatzins are found only in South America. They live in the northern and central part of the continent, throughout the Amazon rain forest.

The Amazon is the largest rain forest on Earth. It is a thick, lush, **tropical** forest that is home to countless plant and animal species.

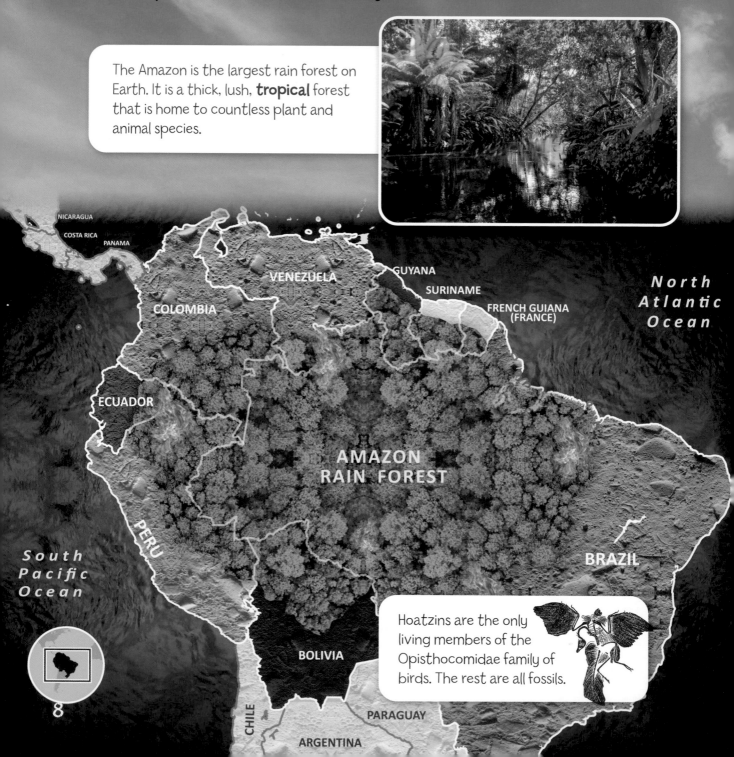

North
Atlantic
Ocean

NICARAGUA
COSTA RICA
PANAMA

VENEZUELA

GUYANA

SURINAME

FRENCH GUIANA
(FRANCE)

COLOMBIA

ECUADOR

AMAZON
RAIN FOREST

PERU

South
Pacific
Ocean

BRAZIL

Hoatzins are the only living members of the Opisthocomidae family of birds. The rest are all fossils.

BOLIVIA

PARAGUAY

CHILE

ARGENTINA

GO CLIMB A TREE

Hoatzins live in trees near water. They make their homes in swamps, flooded forests, and beside lakes and rivers.

LOOKS LIKE RAIN

The **climate** where hoatzins live is very hot and humid. There are two seasons—a rainy season and a dry season. But it rains A LOT all year.

LORD OF THE WINGS

There are thousands of bird species in the world—and none are quite like the hoatzin!

Total bird species on Earth	10,000
Bird species found in South America	3,400
Bird species in the Amazon rain forest	1,300
Bird species found only in the Amazon rain forest	28
Bird species as strange as the hoatzin	0

A Puzzling Bird

Hoatzins have puzzled scientists for years. These odd birds don't quite fit in with other **families**!

FOWL PLAY
For a long time, scientists thought hoatzins were related to chickens, turkeys, and other heavy-bodied ground birds.

GOING CUCKOO
Today, some scientists put hoatzins in a family with cuckoos, roadrunners, and other medium-sized birds.

DOVETAIL
Some scientists put hoatzins in a family with stout-bodied doves and pigeons.

SO LONG
Others think hoatzins belong with long-crested, long-tailed turacos.

FAMILY OF ONE
And some scientists put the one-of-a-kind hoatzin in a family all its own.

BUILD-A-BIRD

What do you get when you combine a chicken, a cuckoo, a cassowary, and a hawk? A puzzling bird like the hoatzin!

guira cuckoo's wild crest

cassowary's blue face

hawk's long, stiff tail

chicken's plump body

Eat Like a Bird

The hoatzin is an oddball in every way. It does not look like other birds. The hoatzin's **digestive system** is also unlike other birds.

LEAF ME ALONE
Most birds eat seeds, fruit, or small animals. Hoatzins eat mainly leaves. They are the only birds in the world with this diet.

TABLE FOR ONE
Hoatzins eat mainly leaves of more than 50 plant species. Few animals can digest, or break down, leaves, so hoatzins do not have to compete for food.

Animals that eat mainly leaves are called folivores.

BITE OR FLIGHT
The hoatzin has a much bigger **crop** than other birds do. Its huge crop leaves little room for flight muscles. That's why this belly-buster of a bird can barely get off the ground!

PIGEON

BUMPER CROP
After a hoatzin eats, the leaves are ground up in a body part called a crop. **Bacteria** in the crop help break down the leaves.

The crop of a typical bird, such as a pigeon, is much smaller than the crop of a hoatzin.

HOATZIN

Upper esophagus
Carries food and liquids to the stomach.

Crop
A pouch joined to the **esophagus**. Food is broken down here.

Stomach
Two sections: proventriculus and **gizzard**.

Proventriculus is a fancy name for the first part of a bird's stomach.

Eat, Sleep, Repeat

Being a folivore is a full-time job! A hoatzin spends its whole day eating and digesting leaves.

REST AND DIGEST
Leaves take a long time to break down. This means the hoatzin spends most of its time resting. Scientists say they rest up to 80 percent of the day!

PARTS FOR PERCHING
Hoatzins **perch** in trees, often in freshwater **mangrove** forests. They lean forward and rest their big bellies on leathery body parts that keep them from tipping over.

LOTS OF LEAVES
Leaves have very few nutrients. Hoatzins must eat many leaves—and buds, roots, shoots, and flowers— each day to get the energy they need.

Nutrients are natural substances in food that living things need to grow and stay healthy.

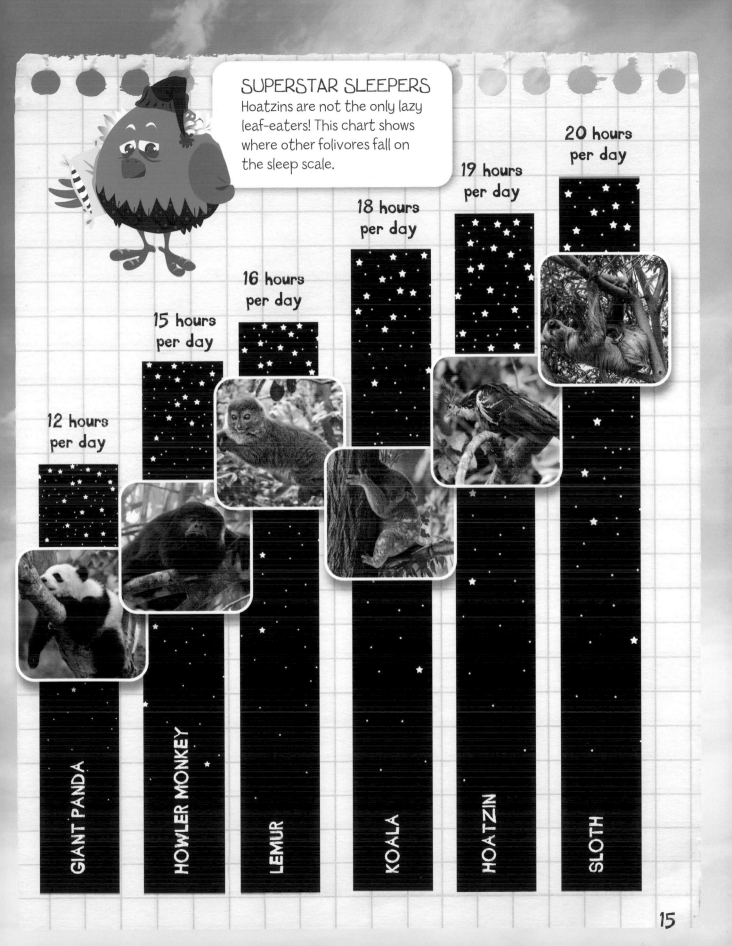

SUPERSTAR SLEEPERS
Hoatzins are not the only lazy leaf-eaters! This chart shows where other folivores fall on the sleep scale.

20 hours per day

19 hours per day

18 hours per day

16 hours per day

15 hours per day

12 hours per day

GIANT PANDA

HOWLER MONKEY

LEMUR

KOALA

HOATZIN

SLOTH

Chicks and Sticks

Hoatzins don't just eat and sleep in trees—they also **breed** and raise their chicks there.

WATER UNDER THE TREE

Hoatzin pairs breed during the rainy season. They build messy stick nests on tree branches that hang over flooded land.

Hoatzins announce their chosen mates and breeding areas with noisy squawks.

Hoatzins are social birds.
They live and nest in small groups.

GET CRACKING

A hoatzin mother lays two or three eggs in the nest. Then both parents, their older chicks, and other hoatzin helpers get cracking!

IT TAKES A VILLAGE

The birds guard and sit on the eggs, which hatch after about a month. Then they protect the helpless, featherless chicks and **regurgitate** leaves for them to eat.

Day 70 to 100: Chicks lose their wing claws

Day 70: Chicks learn to fly

Day 60: Adults stop feeding the chicks

Day 14 to 21: The chicks leave the nest

Day 1: Hoatzin chicks hatch

Stink Birds

Hoatzins seem like sitting ducks. They can barely fly and spend most of the day perched in trees. But hold your nose because these birds have a secret weapon!

SMELL YOU LATER!

The foul smell is the hoatzin's best defense. Few animals will get near this stinky bird, let alone eat it!

HOLY COW!

The bacteria that break down leaves in the hoatzin's body have a nasty odor. It makes the birds smell like fresh cow poop!

SUPER STINKERS

Hoatzins are not the only stinkers in the animal world. Some creatures drop stink bombs to keep **predators** away.

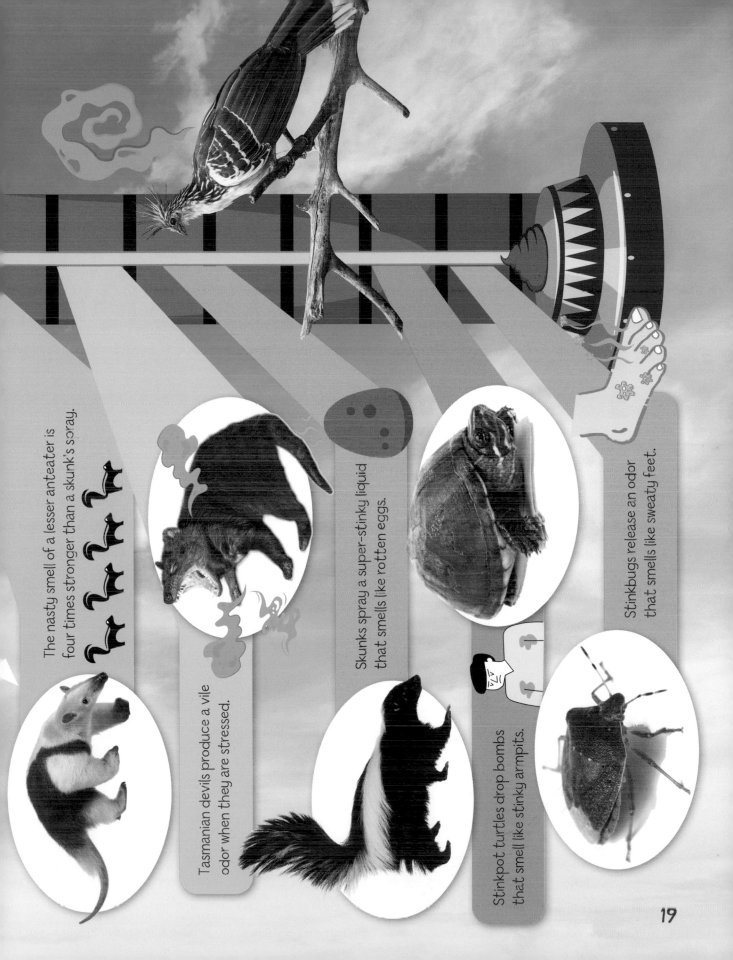

The nasty smell of a lesser anteater is four times stronger than a skunk's spray.

Tasmanian devils produce a vile odor when they are stressed.

Skunks spray a super-stinky liquid that smells like rotten eggs.

Stinkpot turtles drop bombs that smell like stinky armpits.

Stinkbugs release an odor that smells like sweaty feet.

Feast for the Brave

Hoatzins smell awful—and they taste bad too (to humans, anyway). Still, some predators are not afraid of making a meal out of these stinkers.

DONE LIKE DINNER

Adult hoatzins are **prey** for capuchin monkeys and weasel-like animals called tayras (right). Hoatzin chicks are also hunted by snakes and large birds such as hawks.

Dinnertime!

ANGRY BIRDS

When predators get close, adult hoatzins hoot and holler. They flap their wings wildly and crash around in the trees to confuse and scare the predators away.

Auntie is NOT happy!

The Great Escape

While adults distract the predators, hoatzin chicks make their escape.

Step #1

First, the chicks use their wing claws to climb tree branches and hide in leaves.

Step #2

If that doesn't work, the chicks jump out of the trees into the water below.

Step #3

Then, they hide underwater until the danger has passed. (They are excellent swimmers.)

Step #4

Finally, the chicks climb back up the trees and safely into the nests.

Battle of the Birds

Who would win the battle for stranger bird—a hoatzin or a Guinea turaco?

"STINKY FURY" HOATZIN

VS

BIRDS OF A FEATHER
Both are medium-sized birds with supersized crests, short wings, and long tails. They are better at climbing than flying—but are best at sitting and squawking!

TREE-MENDOUS TURACO
The Guinea turaco is found only in Africa. Like the hoatzin, it lives in trees and gathers in small, noisy groups in its habitat.

"GREEN DEATH" TURACO

GO GREEN
Turacos produce a unique bright green color in their feathers. It is the only true green **pigment** in birds. Hoatzins just produce gas.

TURACO TUESDAY
Unlike the leaf-eating hoatzin, the green turaco does not eat its greens. It eats mainly fruit.

TOE-TALLY COOL
Turaco chicks have claws on their wings just like hoatzin chicks do. Turacos can also do a cool feat with their feet. They can turn one of their toes forward to perch or backward to climb trees!

Fact or Fiction?

Hoatzins may seem too weird to be true. Like most odd birds, they are products of millions of years of **evolution** and **adaptations**. This means they have many habits that seem strange.

#1

It takes up to 45 hours for a hoatzin to digest a leafy meal.

FACT!

A hoatzin's crop works overtime to break down tough leaves.

#2

Hoatzins **migrate** long distances to find food and better weather.

FICTION!

These terrible fliers stay put. Their oversized crop means less room for flight muscles. Young hoatzins don't even start flying until they are over two months old, or 65 days!

#3

The hoatzin's nickname is turd bird.

FICTION!

But it has many other great nicknames!

(Flying skunk)

#4

Hoatzin chicks use their wing claws to ride on adult birds.

FICTION!

Helper birds care for young hoatzins, but they don't do piggybacks!

#5

The hoatzin is the national bird of Guyana.

FACT!

They live in the thick forests of the Amazon and Orinoco river basins. Bird watchers flock to South American countries to see this unusual bird in its habitat.

WOW! WHAT A BIRD!

ONE PEOPLE   ONE NATION   ONE DESTINY

Dinosaurs Among Us

Scientists believe that all birds evolved from dinosaurs. But the hoatzin is more dinosaur than most other birds!

OLD BIRD
Some scientists believe hoatzins are the oldest birds in the world. Their ancestors lived 64 million years ago.

FIRST BIRD
The hoatzin is like a small dinosaur called the Archaeopteryx. It had feathers and wings and is considered the first bird to ever live.

Creature Features

ARCHAEOPTERYX

Strange-looking, chicken-sized animal

Claws on its wings for at least part of its life

Can barely fly

Small, sharp teeth for eating meat

Rounded wings and a long tail

Feathers covering its body

Spends most of its time in low tree branches

Died out millions of years ago

HOATZIN

Species change and develop over time to survive in changing habitats.

Bird Watch

Today, hoatzins are not at great risk of dying out like the dinosaurs. But that could change in the future.

GOING DOWN
The exact number of hoatzins is unknown. But scientists do know the **populations** of these birds are decreasing.

SAVED BY THE SMELL
Some people hunt hoatzins and collect their eggs for food. But the rotten smell and bad taste of these birds keep most hunters away.

LOSING THEIR LEAVES

The biggest threat to hoatzins is habitat loss. People cut down trees for lumber. They drain and clear land to build farms and cattle ranches.

20%

People are destroying the Amazon rain forest at an alarming rate. Nearly one-fifth of the forest has been cut down in the past 50 years.

Learning More

Guyana is 85 percent forest.

BE A FRIEND TO HOATZINS

Hoatzins are not endangered birds, but people are working to protect their habitat for the future. Hoatzins need their natural forest environment. They cannot be bred successfully in zoos because it is hard to provide them with the huge number of leaves they need each day. This makes **deforestation** and habitat loss due to **climate change** a threat to them. Luckily, while large parts of the Amazon rain forest are cut down every year, Guyana is one country that is focused on protecting its forests.

You can help hoatzins by learning more about them and the threats they face. Then spread the word and help keep these odd birds going strong!

BOOKS

Farley, Christin. *The Little Book of Animals of the Rainforest: A Guide to Life in Earth's Most Diverse Ecosystem*. Bushel & Peck Books, 2022.

Perdew, Laura. *Spit Nests, Puke Power, and Other Brilliant Bird Adaptations*. Nomad Press, 2020.

WEBSITES

Animal Diversity Web: Hoatzin
animaldiversity.org/accounts/Opisthocomus_hoazin/

Audubon for Kids
www.audubon.org/get-outside/activities/audubon-for-kids

Animalia: Hoatzin Facts
https://animalia.bio/hoatzin

Glossary

adaptations Gradual changes that make a species more suited to its environment

bacteria Very tiny organisms that can be helpful or harmful to living things

breed To produce offspring

climate The normal weather conditions in an area

climate change Long-term changes in Earth's weather patterns

crest A growth of feathers on a bird's head

crop A pouch inside a bird's body used to store and break down food

deforestation The act of cutting down trees and clearing forests

digestive system The connected body parts that take in and break down food

esophagus The tube that carries food from the mouth to the stomach

evolution Changes in a species' characteristics over multiple generations

families Classifications of animals based on shared traits

gizzard The body part in birds that grinds food

mangrove Trees and shrubs that grow in coastal swamps

migrate To move from one place to another seasonally

perch To sit on a high branch or bar

pigment Natural substance that gives color

populations Groups of animals living in certain places

predator An animal that hunts and eats other animals

prey Animals that are eaten by other animals

regurgitate To bring food that has been swallowed back out of the mouth

tropical The areas on Earth near the equator, with hot and humid weather

Comprehension Questions

1. Hoatzin chicks are born with claws on their wings, which they use to _____ .
    a. fight off predators
    b. climb, until they learn to fly
    c. pick up food to eat
2. On what continent are hoatzins found?
    a. Asia
    b. Australia
    c. South America
3. The crop is a body part that allows a hoatzin to _____.
    a. digest leaves
    b. make loud squawking noises
    c. lay eggs
4. True or False: Hoatzins are the only living members of the Opisthocomidae family of birds.
5. True or False: The hoatzin is the national bird of Brazil.

Answers: 1. B, 2. C, 3. A, 4. True, 5. False

Index

ABOUT THE AUTHOR

Robin Johnson is an author and editor who has written more than 100 nonfiction children's books on everything from food scientists to animal celebrities. When she's not working, Robin enjoys playing bird-themed board games with her husband and two sons and has no egrets about using hawkward bird puns.

Crabtree Publishing

crabtreebooks.com   800-387-7650
Copyright © 2024 Crabtree Publishing

In Canada: We acknowledge the financial support of the Government of Canada through the Canada Book Fund for our publishing activities.

Hardcover   978-1-0398-1532-2
Paperback   978-1-0398-1558-2
Ebook (pdf)   978-1-0398-1610-7
Epub   978-1-0398-1584-1

Library and Archives Canada
Cataloguing in Publication
Available at the Library and Archives Canada

Library of Congress
Cataloging-in-Publication Data
Available at the Library of Congress

Published in Canada
Crabtree Publishing
616 Welland Avenue
St. Catharines, Ontario
L2M 5V6

Published in the United States
Crabtree Publishing
347 Fifth Avenue
Suite 1402-145
New York, NY 10016

Author: Robin Johnson
Series research and development:
  Ellen Rodger, Janine Deschenes
Editorial director: Kathy Middleton
Editors: Ellen Rodger, Janine Deschenes
Proofreader: Crystal Sikkens
Design: Margaret Amy Salter

Images
Alamy: Science History Images, p 7 (top right),
All other images from Shutterstock

Printed in the U.S.A./072023/CG20230214